To Be Like a Tree

To Be Like a Tree

Stephanie T. Oliver

Step 3 Publishing
Mt. Juliet, TN 37122

Unless otherwise indicated, all Scripture quotations are taken from the New King James Version of the Bible Copyright © 1979, 1980, 1982 by Thomas Nelson, Inc. Used by permission. All rights reserved

To Be Like a Tree
Copyright © 2008 by Stephanie T. Oliver
All rights reserved
ISBN: 978-0-9821036-0-9
Cover design and layout by:
Angela Jackson and Sally Cramer
Printed in USA
Bethany Press International, Bloomington, MN

Special Thanks to:

Marcus Oliver (the love of my life), Paul and Carolyn Crawford, Faye Rogers, Kelly Simpson and Angela Jackson- for allowing God's perfect love to flow through you all in your support of this project.

Contents

    Introduction 9

    Foreword 11

1. A Seed Planted...................... 13
2. Who were You Created For? 19
3. Wind............................... 25
4. Palm Trees and Cedars 31
5. Fruit................................ 39
6. Maturity and Rings.................. 43
7. SCRIM 47

Introduction

Thank you for allowing me to share in your process of growth and maturity in relationship with God. It has been tremendous step of faith to live up to the challenge of writing this study.

My prayer is that men and women throughout the body of Christ will pursue God with more fervor than they ever thought possible. If we could begin to understand how much God cares for us and how much He desires to be realized through us, we wouldn't go another day in selfish pursuit of our own blessings and promises. We would become robust channels of love and life to all those we influence.

That is the purpose of this book. To set you on a path that leads to unconventional servitude that influences all those around you to a greater love for God through Jesus Christ.

Foreword

Why a tree? Psalms the 1st chapter tells us that "Blessed is the man, Who walks not in the counsel of the ungodly, Nor stands in the path of sinners, Nor sits in the seat of the scornful; But his delight is in the law of the Lord, And in His law he meditates day and night. He shall be like a tree, Planted by the rivers of water, That brings forth its fruit in its season, Whose leaf also shall not wither; And whatever he does shall prosper."

The purpose of a tree is determined in the seed long before it is ever planted. It identifies why the tree was chosen and what it is expected to yield once it is sown in the ground.

Trees are much like people. Their role in their environment grows and matures in the same way as their physical stature and age . All of us have a life purpose, a heavenly reason for our existence on the earth. This purpose has been with us from the time we were conceived in our mother's womb. And only God can cause us to produce that which He created in us.

As we grow and mature we become increasingly aware of the manifold gifts and capabilities that life brings to us. These enable us to enjoy our existence and to show forth the glory of our creator. Our willingness to mature allows us to remain consistently useful regardless of the season, time of life, adversity of circumstance or relational environment in which we find ourselves. It is a wonderful revelation to know that God intends to live through us in every way possible.

This journey of becoming 'Like a Tree' is an exciting process of maturing in your love relationship with God and men- to the point that your life exudes the character of your creator.

1

A Seed Planted

To be like a tree you must first become planted. Our lives are like seeds. God has created us to be these wonderful sources of life for the building of His kingdom. But when we start out it is not always evident what we are to become. We must be willing to enter the process that causes us to grow into a healthy life giving 'tree'.

First you must settle yourself in the soil of God's love and become completely regenerated by His word. The day you chose to embrace the love of Christ you chose to die to your ways and let the miracle of life begin in you.

Look at the process of a seed becoming a seedling: It is basically destroyed from its initial form and from its inside ejects an incredible system of absorption, ingestion, process and growth that eventually breaks through the surface and gains the opportunity to become useful.

In Matthew 13: 31-32 Jesus says, "The kingdom of heaven is like a mustard seed, which a man took and sowed in his field. Which indeed is the least of all the seeds. But when it is grown it is greater than the herbs and becomes a tree so that the birds of the air come and nest in its branches." What a testimony to the potential inside each of us that are a part of the kingdom of heaven.

Our life fulfillment should be attained from this perspective. "Little is much, when God is in it". What area of your life feels like a little mustard seed? What is underneath your surface? The elements of a fruitful existence are already contained in your personality, character and heart. It is this wonderful process of dying to a dormant past, and transforming your mind toward a fruitful future that pushes you beyond where you are to where you are called to be. This kind of yielding determines when and how you emerge from underneath the soil into the visible aspect of God's purpose for your existence in the lives of others.

Every individual we come in contact with should be able to receive from us the very thing that we were created to give….shade, nourishment, relief and rest, in some form or another. What you choose to absorb underneath 'the surface'- will determine how well you grow and how useful you are. Take consideration for where and from whom you have chosen to receive 'nourishment'. The people you listen to, the ideals you embrace, and the environment in which you chose to exist is paramount.

You must seek to gain sustenance from God's word, and then allow your roots to spread deep and wide toward the river of life that exists in

A Seed Planted

His presence. Choose to lend your ear to people and things that manifest the peace, power and presence of God and you will absorb the nutrients that foster these traits in your own life.

Whatever you accept is what you will ingest, what you ingest and absorb into your thinking is what you will eventually produce. Seek to spend time with people that sustain and promote the kind of life you know God created you to lead. Many people chose to remain in destructive circumstances because of fear. Fear of people, change, lack, loneliness. We fear these things because we have chosen to trust in our own limited protection from them. A seedling has no protection beyond its environment once it goes into the ground. It is totally dependent on the Master Gardener to care for it until it is able to weather the elements on its own. A seed planted demonstrates trust in its purest form.

Think about your life. Have you chosen to retain your hardened dried shell, and resist absorbing the love of God out of fear that you won't survive the changes? God is better than that. He doesn't allow death where He hasn't already intended to produce life from it. It is how He functions. But the choice to begin is up to us.

Realize today that God's love for you is already greater than you can imagine. So imagine your greatest love for someone and expect more from God. Make a conscious decision to learn His promises for your life. Once you learn them simply begin to accept them as true. Believe them!! Make practical efforts to govern your choices and actions based on these promises…not your own circumstances or environment. God's reality is so much better than ours. You will find yourself better able to see your life in terms of what God intends for you if you do these things.

God's desire for you is to fully show forth His Glory in the earth. Being planted and choosing to live in the context of His life (not your own self serving ideals) - this is the first step.

Ask yourself these questions:

What thoughts have I chosen to ingest and absorb into my character. Are they consistent with the word of God concerning me?

Do my words reflect that I am planted by the river of life? (Are they helping those around me to live better or do the people that listen to me leave me with a sense of death?)

Remember this:

Take inventory of where you have chosen to plant your thoughts and expectations. Expectations are the results of the thoughts we choose to accept and rely upon.

As a man thinketh so is he… Your thoughts can control the condition of your heart…the condition of your heart will control what you have to say about yourself and those around you.

2

Who were You Created For?

This question can present some heavy internal conflict, especially if we don't understand how to learn God's will for life. How can we really know the answer to this question without the context of our creator and His precious Holy Spirit leading, guiding and teaching us? The answer is in God's word. Our discovery of it is a direct result of how much of our lives can be described or defined by what He says vs. what others have labeled us.

Once we have chosen to accept God's thoughts regarding us (His unconditional love for us, His endowment of our lives with His power and grace, His goodness and mercy that continually follows us, …) we can develop a foundation for how we are to function in our present reality. Do we function for the benefit of ourselves or do we function for the benefit of our Heavenly Father, our Creator? Which element determines our thoughts and our actions?

You have to become settled in a place where you can receive God's word and His desire for your life, you must progress in your confidence toward God and his intentions toward you beyond your own needs to the point of meeting the needs of those you are called to influence.

The purpose of a tree bearing fruit is threefold:

1. to perpetuate the reproductive process,
2. to provide a source of nourishment to those living things that thrive off of its fruit, and
3. to identify that tree among others similar and different.

Your role in showing forth the fruit of God's eternal work in your life is to first be able to help others develop the same kind of thriving relationship with your Savior that you have. We all have the ministry of reconciliation; we all have a responsibility to love God in a way that compels others to love Him. What life choices have you pursued that accurately show forth the influence of God's love and His word in your life?

To be effective in this you must understand the timing (season) and array of circumstances in which God created you to thrive. Galatians 5:22-23 tells us: "But the fruit of the spirit is love, joy, peace, longsuffering, kindness, goodness, faithfulness, gentleness, self-control, Against such there is no law." The wonderful thing about 'bearing fruit' is that it is an almost effortless result of being planted in a place where the 'water' of God's Holy Spirit, and the nutrients of His word can be absorbed and converted to relevant life choices. The joy, peace, kindness, longsuffering, faithfulness, gentleness, self-control that we are expected to produce will come forth at the right time if we simply remain planted.

You can't allow anything or anyone to disconnect you from your source of life. When others can experience these wonderful traits in their relationship with you they are drawn to you. As people participate in conversation and interaction with you they are able to experience the difference that His love makes in your character—your fruit, your results. This becomes a magnet opportunity for you to reproduce the love of God in their lives even to the point of seeing them planted beside you.

Your second role in producing fruit is to provide a source of nourishment to those you have been called to serve. This may be a group in your local church, your neighborhood, workplace, or family. You have something to offer. God has a specific people that your life is equipped to serve. **Your significance in the Kingdom of God and on earth can be directly measured by the quality of character you present to those in need of your 'fruit'.** You can think of your fruit as your time, your money, your ideas, your skills…**whatever God's love in you has produced for you, is fruit**.

We should always acknowledge that we are useful to God beyond ourselves. If fruit stays on the branch long after it is ripened it begins to rot. It will lose its opportunity to bring life to something other than itself. Don't lose the opportunity that God has given you to produce life in those around you.

Let's not be selfish with these things and let our fruit remain on the branch and rot. Selfishness breeds fruit that can't be used by others…when it is not useful to those that were created to thrive on it, it will become rotten and eventually die off the branch. You will find that you no longer possess it. **Don't sacrifice God's results in your life because you are not willing to invest them into the lives of others.** If He is your source you never have to worry about losing more than He can replace

The third element of bearing fruit in season is to know that you were created individually and carefully by an incredibly capable God. **Let your identity and value come from what He put inside you…not what others find and receive from you**. I have seen many people find their worth and identity in situations and relationships that only change and sometimes fade. Their job, their family, their children, spouse, friends, hobbies-whatever…these things become the source of their identity and value. God wants you to know who you are in Him, long before anyone else has a clue. This is what happens during the 'down' or dormant seasons in life. On the outside it may seem that the fruit of your life is not yet shown, but remain patient. Timing is everything. God knows that if you show forth certain fruit in the winter it will not survive the elements and be a complete waste of energy. Trust his timing, stay under the control and guide of His word and leave the timing to Him.

Ask yourself this question:

Where do you find your value? Is it in the things and people that surround you, or is it in the one and only one that has the ability to give you everything for life?

Remember this:

Ecclesiastes 3:1 tells us: "To everything there is a season, a time for every purpose under heaven." God has promised to work everything for our good...Trust Him.

3

Wind

One interesting fact about trees is their seeming vulnerability to the elements never seems to stop their productivity. Actually they have learned to take their environment and utilize it to their benefit. When David describes a tree whose leaves shall not whither, he is referring to the sustainability of that tree and its ability to consistently find nourishment and purpose regardless of the season and circumstances.

Have you ever just sat and observed the trees in the wind. They are incredibly resilient and able to bend without breaking. In many instances they can even use the wind to spread their seeds. What if we could respond to the wind with the same kind of wisdom and meekness as the trees?

One of my prayers is for God to grant me a heart to last and a mind to be consistent. When others get to know me regardless of the context, I want them to see Jesus and His awesome work in my heart. Many people find it difficult to be genuine and consistently productive in their lives and in their relationship with others. We often deal with others out of our emotions and feelings, rather than the redeemed spirit of God that dwells in us. If we were to deal with our relationships and circumstances from the perspective of God's design, it would change our ability to remain in times of difficulty. Fair-weather spouses, good time buddies, whatever you chose to call it; if consistency and loyalty is not a part of our character, how will we ever grow to any level of maturity in our relationship with God and others. Too many Christians have forgotten that God's word shows us long suffering, longevity, stamina and consistency is possible in the context of His word and our constant attention upon what <u>He</u> says.

That sounds so simple, but really- How? How do I conform my will and my desires enough to bend to the wind of the Holy Spirit without breaking? How does a tree exercise this kind of strength? By securing itself in the ground deep and wide. It is not enough for the tree to seek water from one direction. **Its stability is a result of its aggressive pursuit of water and its upright posture to make sure it receives the sun. You must actively, deliberately pursue the word of God and keep yourself exposed to the love of Jesus.**

Sustainability is the key to long term prosperity. Can you last? It is what separates the winners from those that lost…don't forfeit your purpose and promise in God because you get bored, or tired. Stick with it until it is finished.

It doesn't matter what area of your life in which you wish to prosper. You must learn the art of longevity. **Make choices that promote long term**

influence. Don't let the enemy deceive you into uprooting yourself and aborting your purpose and God given reward because the wind is starting to blow. A tree firmly planted will not let the wind stop it from being productive. It is secure in itself and its creator's placement of it. It may have to bend and sway to maintain its position but it remains.

I can remember when my second child was 5 years of age; he asked to grow some apples. Being the supportive and wonderful mom that I am- I decided that this would be an incredible learning opportunity for him. He could gain a unique understanding about the process of taking energy from the elements and using it to be productive. Nevertheless, we purchased two apple trees and one peach tree (the peach was for his older sister). In the short time before we planted the trees it had become quite windy. The trees refused to stay up. I got very frustrated because the wind kept knocking them down. I soon realized that they were not going to stay up until I had planted them in the ground. The container wasn't weighty enough or dense enough to support the root system. The root system wasn't strong enough to support the tree on its own. Needless to say- I learned more than he did. The trees did not stop falling until we got them in the ground.

Are you so loosely planted that every wind (small or great) has the potential to knock you down? The answer is in the density and strength of your support structure. It is the chemical balance between the soil, rain and sun that gives us nutrients to produce, but it is the process of planting ourselves in stable ground that gives us the longevity necessary for others to benefit from what our lives produce.

Where has God planted you? Do you find yourself eager to move on because the wind has started to blow? Don't run from what seems difficult and potentially damaging. Remain faithful even in adverse circumstances. Use the elements to show forth the Glory of God through your ability to stand.

The Apostle Paul communicated this to us in different terms, "Therefore take up the whole armor of God that you may be able to withstand in the evil day, and having done all, to stand. Stand therefore having girded your waist with truth, having put on the breastplate of righteousness and having shod your feet with the preparation of the gospel of peace: above all, taking the shield of faith with which you will be able to quench all the fiery darts of the wicked one. And take the helmet of salvation and the sword of the spirit which is the word of God: praying always with all prayer and supplication in the Spirit, being watchful to this end with all perseverance and supplication for all the saints- "Ephesians 6:13-18 NKJV God has provided us with everything necessary to survive the elements of our life here on earth.

Ask yourself this question:

What winds of change are blowing in your life?

Are you willing to bend to exercise the longevity that is necessary for your success?

Remember this:

Don't let fear of destruction or change push you to stop nourishing yourself on the word of God 2Timothy 1:7 reminds us, "For God has not given us a spirit for fear, but of power and of love and of sound mind." Remember to stay firmly in the ground of His love, drink the water of His Spirit and stay exposed to the influence of His Son and walk in the promise that whatever you do will prosper.

4

Palm Trees and Cedars

"And whatever he does shall prosper". There is so much teaching that distorts God's intention for His kids when it comes to prosperity. Interesting that this promise only comes after the tree is planted and proven sustainability. We must stop expecting God's order for our lives to be realized through our mindset of immediate gratification. Too many of us want to avoid the process of growth and development that occurs over a period of time, we want to die in the soil and immediately attain everything God has put in us to be, to have and to do. But there is great reward in understanding and submitting to the timing of God and His will to prosper us in every area of our lives.

God has pleasure when we are at peace in our endeavors and relationships. It is His will that whatever we do prosper (Psalm 35:27). Peace and prosperity are often described as the state of being where there is nothing missing or broken; the absence of lack in any form. This reality is available to us through a progressive lifestyle of learning God's word, applying God's word and remaining faithful in it until it produces through us what God intends for us.

Scripture reminds us that prosperity is a result of our appropriating some key truths in our thoughts and actions:

1. **It is God that Gives us the power to create wealth. [Deuteronomy 8:18]** Financial wealth is a creative process by which we invest our seed into God given ideas, organizations, and people; and through faithful investment we begin to harvest the return He has already promised and prepared for us. This return is not a result of those ideas, organizations and/or people, but a result of His generosity and divine purpose for us to live according to His glory and in His image here on earth. Just like a seed dies and becomes a tree through God's divine process, so does our seed invested initiate the divine process of God in our lives.

2. **Diligence to embrace and use the principles He has given us to operate.** There are several promises God gives us to realize His purpose for our health, relationships, families, finances, business ventures and ministries.

3. **True delight in Him.** We must come to God with a genuine trust in Him and all

of His character [King of Kings, Lord of Lords, Almighty, Healer, Provider, Banner, Love, Shield, Refuge, Redeemer, Counselor, Comforter, Power, and so much more. We are forever learning about the awesome nature of the God we serve]

Psalm 92:12 states, "The righteous shall flourish like the palm tree: he shall grow like a cedar in Lebanon" Wow! What a declaration to be able to bloom with the radiance and character of a flourishing palm tree and the coveted Lebanese Cedar. The idea that God desires for us to be the defining element of a beautiful, strong, and long life is almost more than we can comprehend.

God intended for my life to demonstrate His glory in the same manner that a Palm Tree flourishes….BIG. Palm leaves are huge with bold color and are easily and quickly identified. Our lifestyles are often consumed with appearances and making sure that what is seen on the outside gives no reflection of what is on the inside. But those that belong to God are asked to live in a different way. To develop the unique love of God from the inside out- so much so that it cannot be denied as to its existence in your life.

Does your life show forth the influence of God in a bold, colorful and identifiable way? Can those around you tell what kind of environment you were meant to thrive in based on your external disposition? Or maybe you are more like the Cedar…planted of God in places that men would never intentionally place a living plant. Maybe your life represents the tenacity, and Glory of God's strength to produce beauty and life beyond the environment.

The Cedars of Lebanon grow high in the mountains and they are characterized by their scent, their resin (what comes from within them- when cut) and their girth (their stamina to survive men). They became a symbol of wealth, and quality. They were highly sought after for many of their qualities. Many of us shy away from being like the palm and the cedar. We associate humility with shame and forget that there exists an immeasurable quality of life that comes with simple consistency in our character.

True humility is much like this palm that is able to stand high above the ground and spread its leaves large and wide, and produce fruit that cannot be ignored, yet understands the importance of being able to bend when the wind of heaven blows.

Character is really measured in how you respond on the inside to what is happening on the outside. **The cedars respond consistently and predictably not according to the elements, but to the creator and His innate plan for their existence**. This is what God desires for us. To learn to <u>never be ashamed of the way He has made us, to always take the opportunity to bear fruit and make it visible and accessible to all that come into contact with us</u>. He desires for us to never let our surroundings determine our purpose and stability. We have to allow His work in us to sustain us in the winter and promote us in the spring of our lives.

Psalm 92:12 reminds us that we as the righteous were created to 'Bloom Big' and 'Live Wide'. This scripture should provoke us to live in the unshakeable confidence that the God we have chosen to serve intends to live gloriously through us- without fear or shame.

Psalm 92:13-14 further explains that God's intention toward us is for us to develop into a mature representation of His character. He lets us know that there are a few key things that enable us to be like these trees and represent Him in the earth.

We have to be planted. We have to be committed in a place where we can completely let go of who we are to become who God created us to be. This scripture particularly says planted in the house of the Lord. We must find a body of believers and leadership that is able to cover us as the dirt covers a seed during its transformation. A family of leaders that are able to feed us in the context of our need – at whatever stage we enter the ground. Whether we are transplanted, new Christians or mature pillars, we must engage ourselves in the environment that allows us to grow consistently. We must also be willing to endure in that ground long enough to bloom and become useful in the purpose for which God planted us. This is true of our roles in our churches, homes and relationships.

Faithfulness is measured by time. This is perhaps where many of us miss it. Allow the element of time to work on our behalf. We are committed to people and ideas only in the context of how they benefit us. As trees we have to be willing to be committed to our station long enough to bear fruit, give shade or spawn off other trees of our kind.

If you desire to see God's character developed in you to the point of realizing your purpose - remember that becoming planted in the Kingdom of God also means becoming planted in a local church. Don't allow fear and/or pride to cheat you of the stability and growth only found in the context of vibrant relationships with other believers and leaders.

Ask yourself this question:

Where has God planted you?

What body of believers have you committed to remain with and grow?

Can you be described as loyal to the things of God, or do you waiver at the slightest breeze?

Remember this:

It is through the kind of relationships found amongst other believers that we can "pollinate" each other and accelerate our productivity and growth. Christians are not self pollinating trees. We were created to interact and fellowship with others. These interactions develop into relationships through which the fruit of the spirit can be realized and multiplied.

5

Fruit

There are several instances in which Jesus compared our lives to those of fruit bearing vines. Matthew 7:16 states," You will know them by their fruits… Therefore by their fruit you will know them." John 15: 1-8 tells us (Jesus Speaking): " I am the true vine, and My Father is the vinedresser. Every branch in Me that does not bear fruit He takes away……You are already clean because of the word which I have spoken to you. Abide in Me and I in you. As the branch cannot bear fruit of itself, unless it abides in the vine, neither can you, unless you abide in Me. …He who abides in Me , and I in him bears much fruit; for without Me you can do nothing. If anyone does not abide in Me, he is cast out as a branch and is withered…If you abide in Me and My words abide in you, you will ask what you desire, and it shall be done for you. By this My Father is glorified that you bear much fruit; so you will be My disciples."

Though a vine is not exactly the same as a tree their life producing character operates under the same principles. You want to offer some sort of tangible evidence of the life of God flowing through you. Something that others can see, something that even when picked, or removed from you can be used to reproduce the same life giving process somewhere else. Bearing fruit is the one aspect of our life that gives us the potential to regenerate the best of what lives in us.

There are some key things we need to remember in our efforts to be fruitful and regenerate the Love of God in our lives and the lives of others. We should never be afraid for others to approach us, especially when we are productive. **No one can take from us what God does not have the power to reproduce in us over and over again.**

I see many businesses and ministries operate with a fear of losing the results they have worked so hard to attain. I have met many talented, gifted and fruitful individuals that because of this have become very conservative in their release of the Gift of God in them. They only give in measures that are comfortable; for fear that they may not regain what is given. This is not how God desires for us to live.

We should never be afraid to deposit in the lives of others what is ripe and ready for consumption. He will create in us the necessary defenses and protective measures from His word to keep dangerous predators from harming us. As long as we are taking in and utilizing the word of God to produce life in us- no predator natural or supernatural can affect our ability to produce.

Fruit

The danger in holding onto what was intended to share is that it will become overripe and lose its effectiveness or eventually die before it is ever realized by anyone. God intends for us to become an infinite supply of results for His Glory. A tree or vine properly fed, attended to and cared for will produce and reproduce indefinitely, and with each season it has the potential to produce more. This is the kind of abundant life that God intends for us to represent here on earth.

We were created to bear fruit: the fruit of the spirit of God that lives in us (kindness, gentleness, meekness, love, joy, peace, longsuffering and self-control), the fruit of His word manifested in our lifestyle of obedience to Him, and the fruit of our labor in leading and influencing those around us toward a life that pleases God. All of this is possible through our submission to the process of growing and standing. Ingesting the nutrients of Gods wonderful word, absorbing the light, the glory of a Holy God to reflect in our character, committing to endure each season knowing that even in times of dormancy or pruning, God is never remiss to bring what we need so that in due season we can produce and reproduce in a manner that pleases Him.

Ask yourself these questions:

What kind of fruit are you bearing in your life?

Does it provide 'food' that others can ingest and utilize for their own growth- or is it overripe, unpicked and rotting with worms or decay?

Remember this:

The results we experience in God are a byproduct of our ability to absorb, ingest, and reproduce the Word of God, and then depend on the spirit of God and completed work of Jesus Christ to produce in us what ever is necessary for those that He has called us to serve/lead.

6

Maturity and Rings

What will they say of your tree when it is time to cut it down? The maturity of a tree is not often realized until it is cut down and the inner rings are exposed. They reveal the growth pattern of the tree and how it responded each year to its environment. A thin ring represents minimal growth and perhaps reduced exposure to the elements that aid in its growth. A thicker ring can represent significant growth and absorption of proper nutrients of that year. Each ring contributes to the increased viability of the tree and creates a thicker stronger stem through which the tree can feed itself.

How interesting this analogy becomes for our own development and maturing process. Each year we have the potential to show forth a certain amount of growth and maturity, but only if we remain. There is much to be said for a person that has stamina. This character trait is often what separates those that become great influencers and those that barely survive. The ability to last… in whatever element you are planted, through whatever displacements or changes you face….it only becomes relevant if you remain standing.

There is an acronym that I like to use to describe the process of standing, changing, growing and becoming useful in the earth on God's behalf. Each letter identifies a crucial stage in our relationship with God and others. In each stage we experience change, growth and increased productivity for the Kingdom of God.

SCRIM [Salvation, Consecration, Revelation, Implementation, Manifestation]….

Every life must go through these developmental stages repeatedly at every level of growth. Just like a tree when cut reveals its maturity through the number of rings and the depth of those rings; so does the Christian reveal their maturity through the number of times he/she has allowed the ring of SCRIM to be realized in their lives.

Maturity is not solely defined by time but also by evidence. We often confuse time and age with maturity. Many people have chosen to define their maturity by their life experiences. Yet we see as Christians that God does not define it in such terms. He teaches us that **maturity is measured by our relationship with God and our relationship with others. Time is just the element that proves our point.** Those that are growing and maturing in the word of God will remain- "The Survivors".

There is a delicate balance that we must attain where we are able to love the Lord and embrace our responsibility to each other. God has given us a responsibility to love others and to live in a way that esteems them- but <u>never at the expense of time, attention and focus on Him</u>. As a matter of fact He understands that the only way to fully love and serve those around us is to love and serve Him first. This is what the journey is all about. Living life more concerned with manifesting God's Glory more than your own.

Ask yourself these questions:

Do you deliberately manage your day from a perspective of God's Glory?

Or do you schedule your own priorities first then fit God's agenda into your own?

Remember this:

We are planted like seeds into the earth and enter the wonderful cycle of experiences that we call life. These experiences at some point will lead us to our Creator – God. We then enter a decision point where we become a candidate to receive all the blessings and promises intended for us from God. This process of SCRIM helps us to better understand how God accomplishes His will through us and for us.

7

SCRIM

SCRIM: S

Salvation

In John 14:6 Jesus said to him, "I am the way, the truth, and the life. No one comes to the Father except through Me." Every believer by definition has experienced the saving grace, power and love of the precious Son of God- Jesus. This initial experience came as a result of your invitation of Jesus Christ into your life, your heart, your mind – your existence. You invited Him in. For too many Christians this process that initiated their new life stops here.

Salvation is an entire experience. That means that the entirety of what Jesus intends for you is only through your acceptance of Jesus as Lord. He must be allowed to Lord over every challenge you face.

You must allow you entire life to be touched by the redeeming blood of Jesus. Your realization of your own need for salvation doesn't stop after your initial confession. It must become an integral part of your growing relationship with God.

Salvation starts the regeneration deep in your heart to push your life out of the darkness of the soil and expose you to the warmth, and nourishing power of the "Son". In order to pursue and realize your God given destiny and mature in your relationship with Him, **the same sentiments, repentance, and humility that brought you to Him the first time must remain a part of your character through every life circumstance.**

We must always know that no matter what we have encountered in life- only Jesus is able to bring us into a life that is more alive and more fulfilling than before. Only His blood gives us the victory over our adversary and over the world (I John 5, Revelations 12: 11, John 10:10) the same confession (Jesus is Lord) that introduced you into a life a victory is what will cause you to mature and grow in the same. Salvation is a one time experience that initiates in us the process of reliance on Christ to deliver us, equip us, maintain us, and develop us into our destiny.

Ask yourself these questions:

Do you rely on the finished work of God's son Jesus Christ to redeem you or do you rely on your experiences?

Do you consistently acknowledge Jesus as the redeemer in every area of your life?

What areas of your life are left unredeemed?

What part of your seed/life has yet to die and become regenerated by the work of Jesus Christ?

Remember this:

The state of mind and consequence of heart that brings us to God is also what keeps us there. Remaining secure in God's love for us is key to growing, producing and maturing in our Christian experience. Though we die in the soil and break through the ground a new creation...we still remain rooted and grounded in the finished work of the Cross and His resurrection.

SCRIM: C

Consecration

"He who comes to God **must first believe that He is God**..." (Hebrews 11:6 NKJV) How do I get to a place where I can believe? Now that I have accepted that I must learn to fully rely on God – as my true savior. How do I move beyond just depending on him to believing Him; trusting and having full confidence in Him? At what point do I breakthrough the surface of the ground in which I have been planted and start to glorify Him?

There are times in our life where we feel left with no option but to depend on certain people or circumstances. God does not want our relationship with Him to stop just at our acknowledgment of our need for Him. He wants us to believe. To believe means to have a firm religious faith, to accept as true, genuine, or to have a firm conviction as to the goodness, efficacy, or ability of something to hold an opinion: to consider to be true or honest, to accept the word or evidence of, to hold as an opinion.[1] Belief is fostered through a commitment of faith (intangible evidence that what you can't yet see is still true & the only tangible proof that what you hope for will come to past), to trust God unconditionally and without reserve. Consecration gives you the necessary mental/spiritual posture to forgo, forget, and submit your own will to the will of the father. At some point a seedling has to change its posture from the way it was planted to push through the surface and begin to grow upright.

Consecration allows us to separate our thoughts, intents, and desires from our experiences, to the word, purpose, presence, and spirit of God.

Consecration is simply the actions we chose in effort to sanctify or present our lives to God as a living sacrifice.

To consecrate oneself is to make or declare oneself as sacred, set apart, dedicated or devoted to the service and worship of God. It is where we change from being internally focused to an upright pursuit of God through His Son Jesus Christ. Consecration may involve such things as a commitment to fast, or pray or discipline our minds not to participate in activities that may in one way or another overshadow the word of God in our lives. This element prepares our minds to and hearts to receive from God. How much more effective can we become as influencers – as Christians- if we are in a position to hear from the Father. We could actually make decisions that follow His will and purpose for our lives.

This is an opportunity for us to take inventory of what is inside of us and demonstrate our faith in Gods word. Some bible examples of ways that people consecrated themselves unto God include their fasting, prayer, abstinence, speech.

---
[1] Merriam Webster.com

Ask yourself these questions:

What area of your life does not demonstrate true devotion and commitment to God our Father?

In what ways can you practice a lifestyle of consecration?

Remember this:

Simple acts of consecration do not make us more righteous or holy- but they create in us a more malleable surface upon which God can fashion His perfect will for our lives. Consecration is the element of our growth where our posture changes and pushes above the surface into the light.

SCRIM: R

Revelation

"He who comes to God must first believe **that He is God** and that He is a rewarder of them that diligently seek Him." Hebrews 11:6 now you have pushed above the surface and its time to show forth the Glory of God. Do you really know on whom you believe? What are you doing with where God has placed you?

Proximity to the word doesn't insure that you are absorbing and internally applying it to your life. You must become like the tree root system which diligently seeks out the water and instinctively knows how to draw all that it needs to produce external proof of internal sufficiency.

Where do you desire to produce life? Where do you desire to be a place of refreshment and protection for someone around you? This is where you need to seek out God's revealed word to you and understand His nature, His sentiment, His heart toward that particular area of your life. The roots of a tree will extend themselves until they find water. Have you found your source of water- life, Do your spiritual roots have a "seek until you find" tenacity when it comes to receiving the word of God.

God's revealed word. The Bible. Finally you have something more tangible to bank on. You might feel as if it is just a word, nothing you can actually hold. **I challenge you to begin to trust God's word just like you trust that the food you eat on daily basis will keep you alive.**

Your ability to receive God's revelation gives you the foundation from which to make decisions and think. Time spent in and with the word of God is the only sure way to produce viable, fruit. It is the only way to sustain the internal and external integrity of your tree. **What you say and what you do is a byproduct of how much of the revealed word of God you embody within yourself.** You must seek out the word, you must be taught the word. To seek and learn implies that the word extends beyond your cognitive ability to understand the meaning of each phrase. It suggests that you have been able to take it in and manifest it in the way you live.

It can be likened to the minerals in the soil and water that are necessary for you to survive. You will require more and more as you grow and even more as you produce fruit and even more as you remain.

We must remember that fellowship in a local church body that teaches the accurate, balanced word of God is key. Individual time must be a priority; even the 'selfish' aspects of your relationship with God won't last long without the consistent entry of the word of God.

The revelation of God through His word provides the government for your thoughts. Your thoughts determine your actions (As a man thinketh so is he) - your actions reveal you.

Open your heart and your mind to what God has to say to you. When you know that you are ready to receive from God- pull out your bible first. It is your best tool for learning and walking out the will of God for your life.

Ask yourself these questions:

How often do I pursue my answers from the bible?

Do I rely more on my experiences and opinions more than I do on the word of God?

Remember this:

Nothing will accomplish more in your mind and your actions than your decision to pursue God's word concerning your life. Revelation is more than just reading, but embracing the word enough to obey it and live out the results.

SCRIM: I

Implementation

What do you do with what you have been given? To whom much is given much is required. (Luke 12:48)

The will to obey… Will you implement the things that God has been so faithful to show you about yourself? If you have been in church for a while you may have heard the scripture clichéd- "Obedience is better than sacrifice". I can remember my mother often referring to this scripture when I attempted to debate my way out of obeying one of her directives.

I have come to realize that my heavenly Father is much like my earthly mother in his appreciation of my obedience. Many times we are deceived into thinking that somehow our compromise or self denial at some self determined price will compensate for our lack of obedience.

We often feel that our finite methods and habits are more effective than the simple word of God. **A tree that fails to implement or follow through on delivering what it was designed to produce will eventually become useless.** Jesus put it to us like this, "if you love me, then you will keep my commandments." It is more important to God that we simply do as He has instructed us- and let our love be expressed through obedience.

Do you have the ability to obey? Of course you do!! The book of Daniel demonstrates an incredible result from Daniel having not only the willingness to obey God, but the skill and understanding required to obey in a way that influenced others to acknowledge his God. **Such skill and ability was realized through consistent commitment to what he knew pleased God**. At every level he exercised his trust and faith in God (his diet, his prayer life, his relationship with leadership). Daniel did not compromise his trust in God's ability through him. In whatever area you are finding it difficult to obey God. Use Daniel as your example; and seek to trust God in this manner and start with knowing that the skill and ability is not in you, but in God and His loving presence working in and through you.

Ecclesiastes 6:1-2 talks about a man that has received power and wealth and does not gain the benefit of consuming any of it. **Utilizing what God has given us for His glory allows us to adequately consume and effectively share what He puts in us.** This is how we enjoy the process that God allows in our lives. When we are doing the will and word of God – we reap the benefits both immediate and long term. We are able to enjoy growing and giving; not just because we are called to, but more because we understand our own fulfillment is only in being what we were created to be from the beginning.

I remember an individual that used to often discuss how important it is to show love to those that mistreat us. We would get together every so often and discuss how important it was to show love and implement the word of God especially with difficult people. But when it came time to fully embrace the individuals that so badly needed the love of Christ in their lives- we always found it difficult to follow through. We would rather discuss the word of God instead of simply obeying the word of God. We enjoyed the ideals of 1 Corinthians 13- we just chose to not make them a reality in our lives. How much more strength and effort did it take to simply embrace the individuals that were being so rude and ruthless with the same kindness and acts of kindness that we expressed to each other.

Nevertheless God's love prevailed. Our hearts were pricked with compassion and God was able to use us to bring comfort and peace in the midst of a chaotic circumstance.

Why was it so difficult to simply be love? **Somewhere deep in our root system was a dry spot. Somewhere we had failed to pursue God's love for us and His will for us concerning those around us. We relied on our opinions and past experiences more than the word of our Creator.**

Ask yourself these questions:

Have we really gone to God and His word on the matter- is He really lord and savior of that particular area of our lives,

Have we sought to live by the spirit of God and not the Flesh of man- seeking to please God at the expense of self?

Are we listening and paying attention to all that God communicates to us concerning the matter?

Remember this:

Implementing the word of God is not always the easiest thing but it is always the most rewarding. *God's promises often come with conditions. His love comes without condition – but his promises often have prerequisites. Be willing to meet all the prerequisites and you will be able to reap all the benefits. Be willing to only meet some of the prerequisites and you preclude yourself from the fullness of the promise of God in that area.*

Look at the Lebanese Cedars. The maturity and health of that tree depends heavily on the density of the soil in which it exists. It produces a tremendous amount of sap and requires an increasing amount of sun exposure to maintain its character. We as believers are not much different. To mature in our relationship with God, remain healthy in our relationships with each other and grow in character **we need to create an atmosphere that is densely rich with the word of God and generously exposed to the love of God.**

Constantly remind yourself of God's word concerning you and those you influence. Constantly remind yourself that you were created in the image of God and that His love and His character lives in you and is constantly expressed towards you. His love is the sap that we feed on, and its concentration of nutrients to help us is directly related to how much of His word we have ingested. Let the sap that flows through your 'trunk' be rich enough in nutrients to feed every part of your life- leave nothing dry.

SCRIM: M

Manifestation

This is where others are able to actually approach our tree and determine our state of living based on what they see manifested from us, on us and in us. What is manifested in your life, your heart, your emotions, your thoughts? Manifestation is not the only measure of God's presence in our lives, but it is a big indicator of His absence. **Time is usually the ultimate measure of what we will become, but in the process of time there exists a progressive 'proof' of God's perfect work in us.**

The evidence of our faith is shown in our external progression from a selfish, self actualizing relationship with God to the perfect balance of serving the master in His kingdom on His terms for His benefit and our own. The one that truly has a heart to be a life giving source of refreshment and protection to all with whom they come in contact with is the one He likens to a tree. A tree whose leaves do not wither, even in the process of giving, receiving and just being what the creator intended. This level of commitment can seem to be draining and the temptation to avoid releasing the life in you to preserve your longevity is a very real thing. But He is so perfect that He has protected us from even this reality. A tree feeds itself through its leaf system. This is where the food is produced. When this scripture describes a tree whose leaves do not whither and that whatsoever he does shall prosper, it exemplifies that **God in His faithfulness will not cause you to exist in an environment that leaves you lifeless and without your own needs met.** He has already created us with the ability to be everything He expects of us.

Ask yourself these questions:
Do my words nourish those around me?

Does my attitude provide relief to others?

Is my faith and knowledge of the word strong enough to survive inclement circumstances?

Remember this:
Seek to be like a tree with roots deep enough to search out the necessary source of the word of God, strong enough to survive the weather of life, and integrous enough to use its nutrients to continuously, almost predictably produce life that nourishes everything that surrounds it.